WHY ANDREW SURPRISED?

The story about Andrew is taken from The Gospel of John, chapter 6.

(See also Matthew 14, Mark 6 and Luke 9)

When Jesus looked up and saw a great crowd coming towards him, he said to Philip, "Where shall we buy bread for these people to eat?" He asked this only to test him, for he already had in mind what he was going to do.

Philip answered him, "Eight months' wages would not buy enough bread for each one to have a bite!"

Another of his disciples, Andrew, Simon Peter's brother, spoke up, "Here is a boy with five small barley loaves and two small fish, but how far will they go among so many?"

Jesus said, "Make the people sit down." . . . . Jesus then took the loaves, gave thanks, and distributed to those who were seated as much as they wanted. He did the same with the fish.

When they had all had enough to eat, he said to his disciples, "Gather the pieces that are left over. Let nothing be wasted." So they gathered them and filled twelve baskets with the pieces of the five barley loaves left over by those who had eaten.

After the people saw the miraculous sign that Jesus did, they began to say, "Surely, this is the Prophet who is to come into the world."

John 6:5-14, NIV

Why Was Andrew Surprised?

Published by Scandinavia Publishing House
Nørregade 32, DK-1165 Copenhagen K.
Tel.: (45) 33140091   Fax: (45) 33320091
E-Mail: scanpub1@post4.tele.dk

Copyright © 1997, Pauline Youd
Copyright © on artwork 1997, Daughters of St. Paul
Original English edition published by Pauline Books & Media,
50 Saint Paul's Avenue, Boston, USA
Scripture quotations are from the Holy Bible, New International Version,
Copyright © 1973, 1978, International Bible Society
Design by Ben Alex
Produced by Scandinavia Publishing House

Printed in Hong Kong
ISBN 87 7247 043 7

All rights reserved. No part of this book may be reproduced or utilized
in any form or by any means, electronic or mechanical, including
photocopying, recording, or by any information storage and retrieval
system, without permission in writing from the publisher.

WHY WAS ANDREW SURPRISED?

By Pauline Youd
Illustrated by Elaine Garvin

SCANDINAVIA

"Where can we buy enough bread to feed all of these people?" Jesus asked his friend Philip.

The crowd of people had come to hear Jesus teach about God his father. They had listened all day, but now it was suppertime and Jesus knew they must be hungry.

"We can't afford to feed all these people," said Philip.

Andrew heard Philip and Jesus talking.

"There is a boy here who has five little loaves of bread and two small fish," Andrew told them, "but that's all."

"Bring the boy to me," Jesus said to Andrew.

So Andrew brought the boy with his five loaves and two fish to Jesus.

"May I use what you have to feed these hungry people?" Jesus asked him.

The boy smiled and gave his supper to Jesus.

"Tell the people to sit down on the grass," Jesus told his disciples. The people sat down and Jesus prayed. "Thank you, God, for giving us this food," he said.

Then Jesus took the loaves and the fish and gave them to his disciples to give to all the people.

The people ate and ate. Everyone had as much to eat as he or she wanted.

"Take baskets and collect all the leftovers so no food will be wasted," said Jesus.

The disciples collected twelve baskets full of leftovers.

"But we only had five loaves of bread and two small fish," Andrew whispered to Philip.

Andrew was very surprised because Jesus had fed more than 5,000 people with that bread and fish!

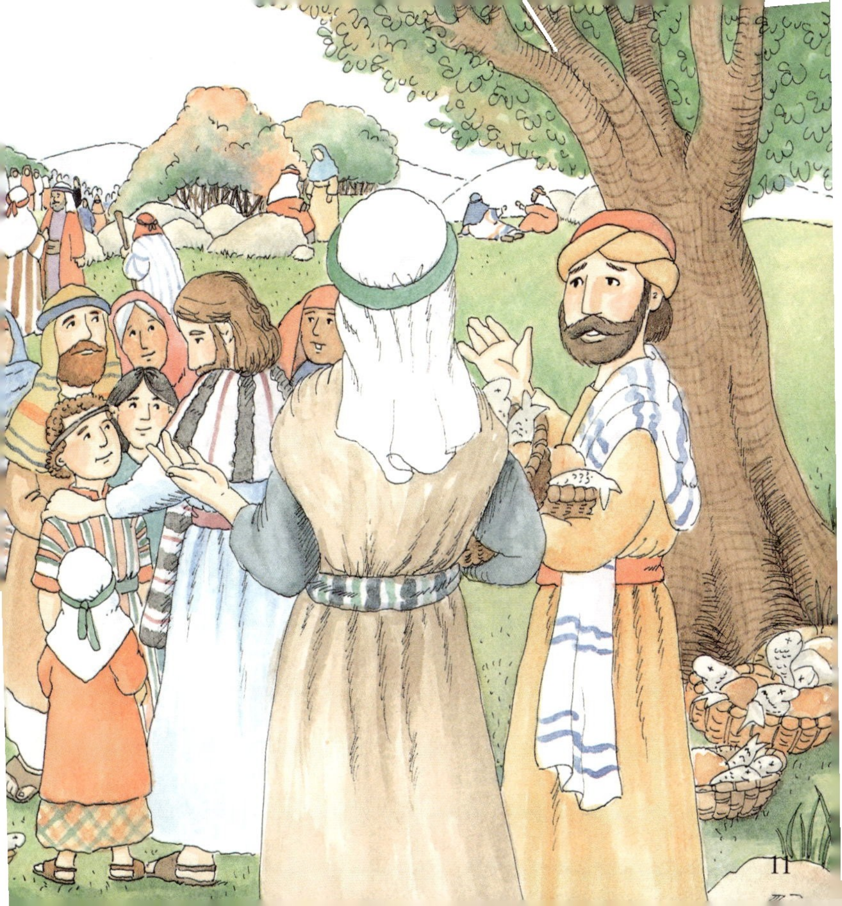

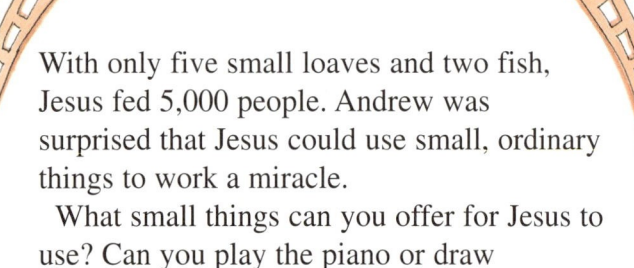

With only five small loaves and two fish, Jesus fed 5,000 people. Andrew was surprised that Jesus could use small, ordinary things to work a miracle.

What small things can you offer for Jesus to use? Can you play the piano or draw pictures? Can you be a peacemaker among your friends? Will you give Jesus part of your weekly allowance by putting it in the collection at church? Give Jesus a helpful attitude at home and watch him work a miracle!

13

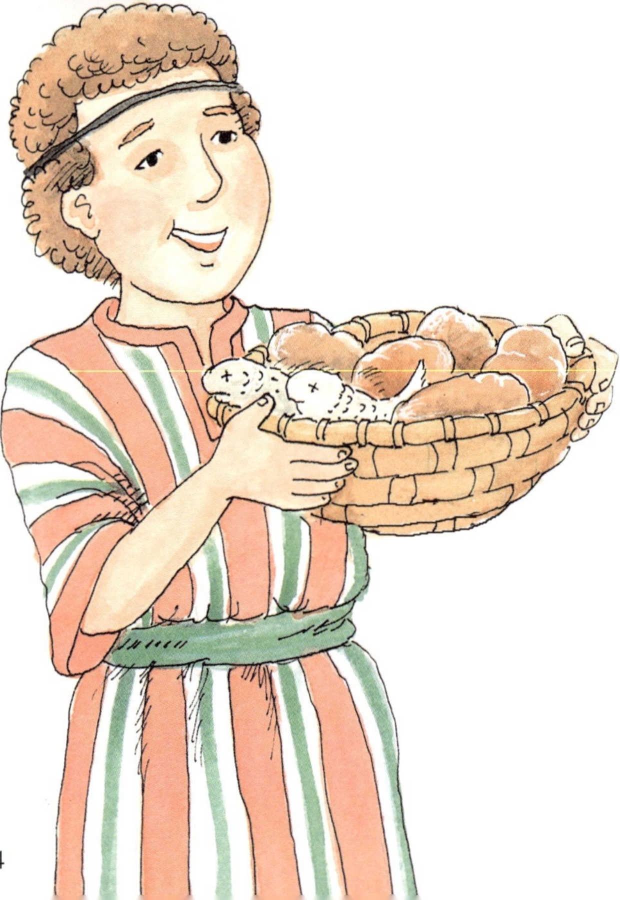

"Here is a boy with five small barley loaves and two small fish, but how far will they go among so many?"
John 6:9

WONDER BOOKS
Lessons to learn from 12 Bible characters

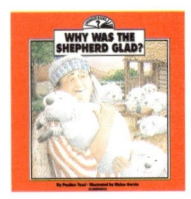

WHY WAS THE SHEPHERD GLAD?	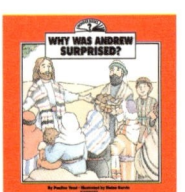 **WHY WAS ANDREW SURPRISED?**	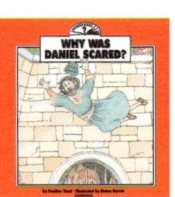 **WHY WAS DANIEL SCARED?**	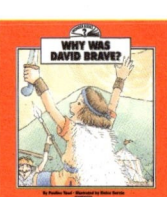 **WHY WAS DAVID BRAVE?**
God's Love	Self-giving	Prayer Overcomes Fear	Praising God
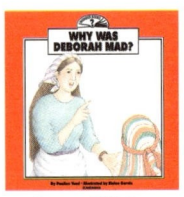 **WHY WAS DEBORAH MAD?**	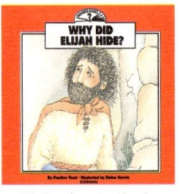 **WHY DID ELIJAH HIDE?**	 **WHY WAS GIDEON WORRIED?**	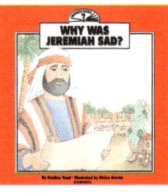 **WHY WAS JEREMIAH SAD?**
Prayer Obtains Wisdom	Listening to God	Trust	Perseverance
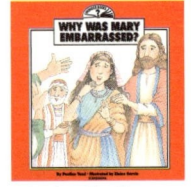 **WHY WAS MARY EMBARRASSED?**	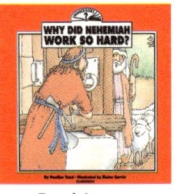 **WHY DID NEHEMIAH WORK SO HARD?**	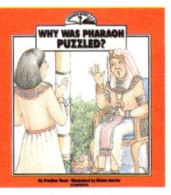 **WHY WAS PHARAOH PUZZLED?**	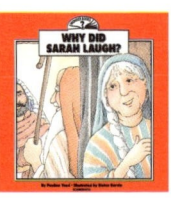 **WHY DID SARAH LAUGH?**
Loving Obedience	Persistence	Asking Advice	Trusting God's plan